Story Prompts
Romance

The Art of Writing Love Stories

Created by Mark El-Ayat

Mark El-Ayat Publishing
Email: Admin@markelayat.com
Website: Markelayat.com

Publisher logo:

Book cover by Mark El-Ayat

First Edition

ISBN: 979-8-9889467-0-0

Printed in United States of America

Year of Publication: 2024

Introduction

Welcome to Story *Prompts: Romance – The Art of Writing Love Stories*, a sanctuary where your passion for romance and storytelling converges. Created for dreamers and writers like you, this book is a gentle nudge into the world of romantic fiction, a realm where every heartbeat and whispered word creates a narrative of love.

Every great love story is fueled by the excitement of new beginnings, the intensity of profound connections, and occasionally, the melancholic ache of separation. Whether you are writing your very first love story or you are an experienced writer of heartwarming tales, these prompts will be your helpful guides along the way.

Within these pages, you will discover an array of prompts, each a seedling awaiting your creative touch to blossom into a full-fledged romance narrative. This course will delve into the nuances that make writing about romance both universally understood and uniquely complex.

The educational material scattered throughout aims to enhance your comprehension and enjoyment of romantic storytelling. Discover the art of creating captivating love stories with these valuable tips, which will empower you with the understanding to master character chemistry and skillfully weave intricate plots.

You may be asking yourself how to use this book. Let it be your daily writing practice, your brainstorming buddy, or your inspirational muse. The prompts are designed to be flexible, allowing you to either follow them to the letter or to veer off into the uncharted territories of your imagination. Accompanying each prompt are pages for you to scribble down thoughts, sketch out scenes, and develop characters. This is your safe space to experiment, explore, and express your storytelling prowess.

As the creator of this series, I invite you to join me in celebrating the art of crafting love stories, to embrace the challenge and joy of writing, and to share your own tales of romance that resonate with the heart.

Plot Outlines

To write a romance story, you'll need to be creative. Before each prompt lies a Plot Outline template and Character Development sheets. To organize your story, I recommend being concise when writing it out and using the Notes section to provide additional details.

Plot Outlines are your blueprints, offering a structured approach to bring together romance, conflict, and resolution, ensuring your tale unfolds with intention and emotional depth.

Within these pages lies a flexible framework adaptable to any romance narrative. Each segment of the Plot Outline helps chart the key milestones of your story, guiding you through the initial spark, the challenges faced, and the ultimate climax that defines the fate of your characters' love.

The Plot Outlines section empowers you to dream, plan, and create a love story that resonates deeply, laying the groundwork for each story and move the heart. Consider this section your invitation to plan your story's course thoroughly, providing a holistic approach to your narrative.

The classic 3-act structure is chosen for romance storytelling for its proven effectiveness in delivering clear, engaging narratives. It offers a straightforward roadmap, dividing the story into setup, confrontation, and resolution, which simplifies complex character and plot development.

This structure adeptly builds emotional depth and tension, essential for the romantic genre, guiding readers through a satisfying journey of love, conflict, and resolution. While providing a structured approach, it also allows for creativity, making it a versatile foundation for a wide range of romance stories.

Employing this structure helps ensure that the emotional journey is coherent and impactful, resonating universally with readers' experiences and expectations.

Character Development

Character development is the backbone of any memorable story. It's through these well-crafted personas that your story will unfold, drawing readers into a world where every glance, every word, and every heartbeat matters. The sheets provided are designed to guide you in exploring the depths of your characters' souls, from their deepest desires to their darkest fears, their quirkiest habits to their most profound beliefs. These explorations will not only provide insights into how your characters handle the ups and downs of love, but will also add genuine emotional depth to your story.

Remember, the most engaging characters are those that feel real and relatable. They are flawed, they grow, and they surprise us. When you thoroughly explore their development from the start, you establish the perfect conditions for a love story that enthralls and lasts.

In crafting a romance story, the depth and relatability of your characters can turn a simple love story into an unforgettable journey.

Use the character sheets to describe both love interests.

The Character Development Sheets are designed to help you flesh out your romantic protagonists and their love interests in detail. Here's what these sheets should include:

Basic Information: Start with the basics—names, ages, occupations, and physical descriptions. This foundational information sets the stage for deeper exploration.

Backstory: Talk about each character's past, including family dynamics, formative experiences, and previous relationships. Understanding where your characters come from informs their motivations and reactions within the story.

Personality Traits: Detail their personalities, from strengths and weaknesses to likes and dislikes. Consider how these traits affect their approach to love and relationships.

Goals and Motivations: What do your characters want, both outside of and within the context of their romantic relationship? Understanding their goals can help drive the narrative forward.

Fears and Flaws: Explore their vulnerabilities and the obstacles they must overcome, both internally and externally. Romantic tension often stems from characters confronting and growing through their fears and flaws.

Relationship Dynamics: Define the dynamic between your characters. Are they opposites that attract, or do they share a deep, fundamental connection from the start? How do their backgrounds and personalities clash or complement each other?

Character Arc: Map out how each character evolves throughout the story. Consider how their experiences in the story, especially their romantic experiences, contribute to their growth.

Dialogue Styles: Note any unique speech patterns, phrases, or words each character might use. This helps in writing authentic and distinct dialogue for each character

Let these Character Development Sheets be the foundation upon which your stories of love, loss, passion, and transformation are built.

Your journey begins here.

The Subgenres

Historical Romance

Delve into the enthralling world of Historical Romance, where the richness of history meets the warmth of love stories. This subgenre invites readers to journey through time, experiencing romance amidst the backdrop of significant historical events and eras. From the opulent courts of medieval kingdoms to the intricate social dances of Regency England, Historical Romance intertwines factual history with the allure of romantic fiction.

Key Elements:

- Authentic Period Details: The charm of Historical Romance lies in its meticulous depiction of the era it's set in, including accurate portrayals of customs, fashion, and social norms.

- Cultural and Social Context: Understanding the societal norms and expectations of the time is crucial in crafting believable and engaging narratives.

- Romance Across Time: These stories often explore how love and relationships were influenced and shaped by historical circumstances.

Notable Works and Authors:

1. *Pride and Prejudice* by Jane Austen: A timeless classic, this novel is set in the Regency era and is renowned for its witty exploration of manners, marriage, and the role of women in early 19th century England.

2. *Jane Eyre* by Charlotte Brontë: While more of a Gothic romance, this novel is significant for its historical setting and strong, complex characters. It offers a profound look at love, morality, and social class in Victorian England.

3. *A Knight in Shining Armor* by Jude Deveraux: A bestseller that blends time travel with historical romance, offering a compelling love story set between contemporary times and Elizabethan England.

4. *Outlander* by Diana Gabaldon: Although already mentioned, it's worth reiterating the impact of this series, which masterfully combines historical fiction, romance, and elements of fantasy.

5. *The Bronze Horseman* by Paullina Simons: Set during World War II in Russia, this novel explores an epic love story amidst the backdrop of a world at war, providing a poignant look at the endurance of love through history's hardest times.

Writing Tips:

- **Research is Key:** Spend time researching the era to ensure authenticity in your story. This includes understanding the language, clothing, and societal structures of the time.

- **Balancing Fact and Fiction:** While historical accuracy is important, remember that the heart of your story is the romance. Find a balance between educating your readers about the period and developing your romantic plot.

- **Character Development:** Create characters that are true to their time but also relatable. Their struggles, desires, and romances should reflect the historical context while resonating with modern readers.

Plot Outline Template

Title: _____

Setting: _____

Theme: _____

Act 1: Setup

• Introduction to Characters: _____

• Inciting Incident: _____

• Establishing Stakes: _____

Key Elements:

• Initial attraction or conflict

• Setting the tone and pace

Act 2: The Confrontation

• Deepening Complications: _____

• Midpoint: _____

• Build-Up to Crisis: _____

Key Elements:

• The evolution of the romantic relationship

• The introduction of secondary conflicts or subplots

Act 3: The Resolution

• Climax: _____

• Falling Action: _____

• Denouement/Conclusion: _____

Key Elements:

• Resolution of the romantic and main story conflict

• Reflection on the journey and growth of the characters

Character Development Sheet

Character Names: _____ / _____

• Nicknames: _____ / _____

• Ages: _____ / _____

• Occupations: _____ / _____

• Physical Descriptions: _____ / _____

• Distinguishing Features (e.g., scars, tattoos):

_____ / _____

Backstory

• Family Background: _____ / _____

• Education & Career Path: _____ / _____

• Significant Past Events: _____ / _____

• Socioeconomic Status: _____ / _____

Personality

• Dominant Traits: _____ / _____

• Fears: _____ / _____

• Desires: _____ / _____

• Hobbies/Interests: _____ / _____

• Habits (good and bad): _____ / _____

• Values & Beliefs: _____ / _____

Relationships

• Current Family Dynamics: _____ / _____

• Friendships: _____ / _____

• Past Romantic Relationships: _____

Goals

• Personal Aspirations: _____ / _____

• Professional Ambitions: _____ / _____

• Romantic Desires: _____ / _____

Conflict

• Internal Conflicts (psychological struggles, fears, uncertainties):

_____

_____

• External Conflicts (with other characters, society, environment):

_____

_____

Character Arc

• Beginning State (personality, situation at the story's start):

_____

_____

• Growth Points (key moments of change):

_____

_____

• End State (transformation or realization by the end):

_____

_____

Dialogue Style

• Speech Patterns (formal, casual, idiosyncratic phrases):

_____ / _____

• Voice (how the character's personality is reflected in dialogue):

_____ / _____

Notes

The Prompt

During the Gilded Age in New York City, a young woman from a humble upbringing and a wealthy, experienced man discover an unexpected romance in the rapidly changing city.

Contemporary Romance

Explore the captivating world of Contemporary Romance, a genre that beautifully portrays the complexities of modern love and relationships. These stories take place in modern settings and accurately depict the challenges of dating, relationships, and personal hardships. This subgenre provides a platform for a wide variety of stories, ranging from delightful romantic comedies to deep and contemplative love stories.

Key Elements:

- Modern-Day Settings: Stories are set in the present day, making them relatable to the contemporary reader.

- Realistic Characters and Situations: Characters deal with current issues, lifestyles, and societal norms, often reflecting the complexity of modern relationships.

- Emotional Depth: While the tone can vary widely, from playful to intense, contemporary romances often explore deep emotional development and personal growth.

Notable Works and Authors:

1. *It Ends with Us* by Colleen Hoover: A poignant and heartfelt story that delves into challenging themes, offering a raw and honest look at love and relationships.

2. *The Hating Game* by Sally Thorne: A witty and engaging workplace romance that explores the thin line between love and hate, featuring two competing protagonists with sparkling chemistry.

3. *Red, White & Royal Blue* by Casey McQuiston: An uplifting and charming tale that combines romance with political and cultural themes, focusing on a relationship between the First Son of the United States and the Prince of Wales.

4. *Normal People* by Sally Rooney: A thought-provoking novel that examines the complexities of modern love and the profound connection between two individuals as they navigate adulthood.

5. *Beach Read* by Emily Henry: A light and heartwarming story about two writers with opposite approaches to life and writing, finding common ground and unexpected romance.

Writing Tips:

- **Authenticity in Characters and Dialogue:** Focus on creating realistic, well-rounded characters whose behaviors and dialogues resonate with the contemporary setting. Authenticity in how characters interact and express themselves is crucial for engaging the modern reader.

- **Balancing Romance and Realism:** While the romantic relationship is central, it's essential to weave in realistic life challenges. This could include career struggles, personal growth, or navigating social issues, providing a richer backdrop for the romance.

- **Diversity and Inclusion:** Reflect the diversity of modern society in your characters and their relationships. Including a range of backgrounds, experiences, and perspectives not only adds depth to your story but also appeals to a broader audience.

Plot Outline Template

Title: _____

Setting: _____

Theme: _____

Act 1: Setup

• Introduction to Characters: _____

• Inciting Incident: _____

• Establishing Stakes: _____

Key Elements:

• Initial attraction or conflict

• Setting the tone and pace

Act 2: The Confrontation

• Deepening Complications: _____

• Midpoint: _____

• Build-Up to Crisis: _____

Key Elements:

• The evolution of the romantic relationship

• The introduction of secondary conflicts or subplots

Act 3: The Resolution

• Climax: _____

• Falling Action: _____

• Denouement/Conclusion: _____

Key Elements:

• Resolution of the romantic and main story conflict

• Reflection on the journey and growth of the characters

Character Development Sheet

Character Names: _____ / _____

• Nicknames: _____ / _____

• Ages: _____ / _____

• Occupations: _____ / _____

• Physical Descriptions: _____ / _____

• Distinguishing Features (e.g., scars, tattoos):

_____ / _____

Backstory

• Family Background: _____ / _____

• Education & Career Path: _____ / _____

• Significant Past Events: _____ / _____

• Socioeconomic Status: _____ / _____

Personality

• Dominant Traits: _____ / _____

• Fears: _____ / _____

• Desires: _____ / _____

• Hobbies/Interests: _____ / _____

• Habits (good and bad): _____ / _____

• Values & Beliefs: _____ / _____

Relationships

• Current Family Dynamics: _____ / _____

• Friendships: _____ / _____

• Past Romantic Relationships: _____

Goals

• Personal Aspirations: _____ / _____

• Professional Ambitions: _____ / _____

• Romantic Desires: _____ / _____

Conflict

• Internal Conflicts (psychological struggles, fears, uncertainties):

_____

_____

• External Conflicts (with other characters, society, environment):

_____

_____

Character Arc

• Beginning State (personality, situation at the story's start):

_____

_____

• Growth Points (key moments of change):

_____

_____

• End State (transformation or realization by the end):

_____

_____

Dialogue Style

• Speech Patterns (formal, casual, idiosyncratic phrases):

_____ / _____

• Voice (how the character's personality is reflected in dialogue):

_____ / _____

Notes

The Prompt

An unexpected romance blossoms between a local barista and a foreign exchange student. As they explore their cultural differences, they find common ground in their shared dreams and values.

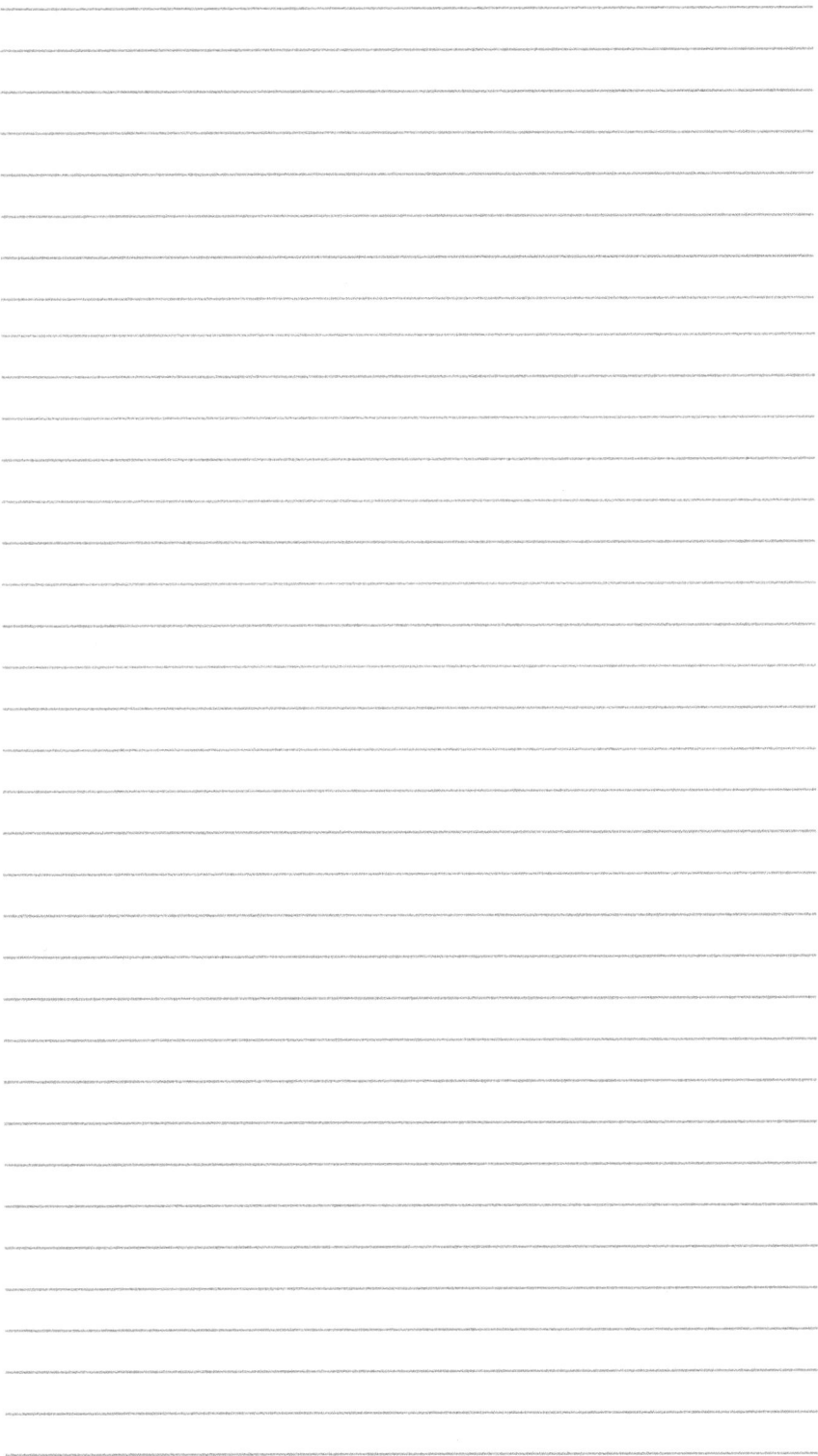

Romantic Comedy

Step into the light-hearted and often hilariously unpredictable world of Romantic Comedy. Rom-Coms combine the warmth of romance with the wit and humor of comedy, creating stories that are as heartwarming as they are entertaining. Set against a variety of backdrops, from the city life to a quaint small-town, these narratives often revolve around quirky characters, amusing misunderstandings, and charmingly awkward situations leading to love.

Key Elements:

- <u>Humor and Wit:</u> The lifeblood of a Rom-Com is its humor, which can range from subtle and dry to outright slapstick.

- <u>Relatable Characters:</u> Characters in Rom-Coms are often everyday people that audiences can easily relate to, with their flaws and all.

- <u>Engaging Plot:</u> Typically involves romantic misunderstandings, serendipitous encounters, or a series of comedic events bringing the characters together.

Notable Works and Authors:

1. *To All the Boys I've Loved Before* by Jenny Han: A sweet and humorous tale of a teenage girl whose secret love letters get sent out to her past crushes, leading to unexpected romantic entanglements.

2. *Can You Keep a Secret?* by Sophie Kinsella: This novel combines humor and romance, following the story of a woman who spills all her secrets to a stranger on a plane, only to find out he's her company's CEO.

3. *The Rosie Project* by Graeme Simsion: A charming story about a socially awkward genetics professor who creates a scientific survey to find the perfect wife but finds an unexpected connection with Rosie, who is the opposite of what he thinks he wants.

4. *Bet Me* by Jennifer Crusie: This book is a heartwarming and funny story about a woman who accepts a bet to date a man she despises, only to find out that love can be unpredictable.

Writing Tips:

- **Balance Humor and Heart:** The key to a successful Rom-Com is striking a balance between humor and emotional depth. Your story should make readers laugh, but also care deeply about the characters and their journey.

- **Create Relatable Characters:** The protagonists of your Rom-Com should be relatable and likable. Quirky traits, awkward moments, and genuine emotions can make characters feel more real and endearing.

- **Inventive and Engaging Plot:** Rom-Coms often rely on unique situations or comedic misunderstandings to drive the story. Be creative with your scenarios but ensure they remain plausible and engaging.

- **Snappy and Witty Dialogue:** Sharp, witty dialogue is a hallmark of Rom-Coms. It should feel natural, enhance the humor, and reveal character dynamics.

Plot Outline Template

Title: _____

Setting: _____

Theme: _____

Act 1: Setup

• Introduction to Characters: _____

• Inciting Incident: _____

• Establishing Stakes: _____

Key Elements:

• Initial attraction or conflict

• Setting the tone and pace

Act 2: The Confrontation

• Deepening Complications: _____

• Midpoint: _____

• Build-Up to Crisis: _____

Key Elements:

• The evolution of the romantic relationship

• The introduction of secondary conflicts or subplots

Act 3: The Resolution

• Climax: _____

• Falling Action: _____

• Denouement/Conclusion: _____

Key Elements:

• Resolution of the romantic and main story conflict

• Reflection on the journey and growth of the characters

Character Development Sheet

Character Names: _____ / _____

• Nicknames: _____ / _____

• Ages: _____ / _____

• Occupations: _____ / _____

• Physical Descriptions: _____ / _____

• Distinguishing Features (e.g., scars, tattoos):

_____ / _____

Backstory

• Family Background: _____ / _____

• Education & Career Path: _____ / _____

• Significant Past Events: _____ / _____

• Socioeconomic Status: _____ / _____

Personality

• Dominant Traits: _____ / _____

• Fears: _____ / _____

• Desires: _____ / _____

• Hobbies/Interests: _____ / _____

• Habits (good and bad): _____ / _____

• Values & Beliefs: _____ / _____

Relationships

• Current Family Dynamics: _____ / _____

• Friendships: _____ / _____

• Past Romantic Relationships: _____

Goals

• Personal Aspirations: _____ / _____

• Professional Ambitions: _____ / _____

• Romantic Desires: _____ / _____

Conflict

• Internal Conflicts (psychological struggles, fears, uncertainties):

_____

_____

• External Conflicts (with other characters, society, environment):

_____

_____

Character Arc

• Beginning State (personality, situation at the story's start):

_____

_____

• Growth Points (key moments of change):

_____

_____

• End State (transformation or realization by the end):

_____

_____

Dialogue Style

• Speech Patterns (formal, casual, idiosyncratic phrases):

_____ / _____

• Voice (how the character's personality is reflected in dialogue):

_____ / _____

Notes

The Prompt

Two high-rise neighbors, one carrying an abnormally large package and the other a self-help book, meet for the first time stuck in an elevator. How does this unfortunate mishap lead them to romance?

Young Adult Romance

Explore the vibrant and emotionally resonant world of Young Adult (YA) Romance, where stories of first loves, self-discovery, and young adulthood come to life. YA Romance often captures the intensity and innocence of young love, through coming-of-age challenges. These narratives resonate deeply with readers, exploring themes like identity, belonging, and transformation through the lens of romantic experiences.

Key Elements:

- Emotional Intensity and Authenticity: The emotional experiences in YA Romance are often intense and portrayed with a sense of authenticity that resonates with young readers.

- Coming-of-Age Themes: These stories typically involve characters navigating the complexities of adolescence and young adulthood, often intertwined with the exploration of romantic feelings.

- Relatable Characters and Situations: Characters in YA Romance are usually teenagers or young adults facing relatable challenges such as school, family dynamics, and societal expectations.

Notable Works and Authors:

1. *The Fault in Our Stars* by John Green: A poignant and touching story of love and life, marked by its sincere portrayal of young romance in the face of adversity.

2. *Eleanor & Park* by Rainbow Rowell: A tender and unique love story about two misfit teenagers discovering first love in the 1980s.

3. *The Sun Is Also a Star* by Nicola Yoon: A poignant and beautifully written novel about a serendipitous encounter between two teens in New York City, exploring themes of fate, love, and existential questions.

4. *Fangirl* by Rainbow Rowell: Cath, an introverted fanfiction writer, navigates her first year of college, struggling with new challenges, an evolving family dynamic, and the complexities of romance outside her beloved fandom.

5. *Anna and the French Kiss* by Stephanie Perkins: Set in Paris, this book is a delightful and romantic story of an American girl finding love and adventure in a new city.

Writing Tips:

- **Capturing the Voice of Youth:** Write in a voice that authentically represents the young adult perspective. The dialogue and narrative should reflect the way young people think, feel, and speak.

- **Addressing Real Issues:** Incorporate themes relevant to young adults, such as self-discovery, family and peer relationships, and the challenges of growing up.

- **Building Emotional Depth:** YA Romance should dive deeply into the emotional lives of the characters. Explore the complexities of young love, including the joy, uncertainty, and intensity that come with it.

- **Avoiding Patronizing Tones:** Treat young adult themes with respect and seriousness, avoiding a condescending or overly simplistic approach.

Plot Outline Template

Title: _____

Setting: _____

Theme: _____

Act 1: Setup

• Introduction to Characters: _____

• Inciting Incident: _____

• Establishing Stakes: _____

Key Elements:

• Initial attraction or conflict

• Setting the tone and pace

Act 2: The Confrontation

• Deepening Complications: _____

• Midpoint: _____

• Build-Up to Crisis: _____

Key Elements:

• The evolution of the romantic relationship

• The introduction of secondary conflicts or subplots

Act 3: The Resolution

• Climax: _____

• Falling Action: _____

• Denouement/Conclusion: _____

Key Elements:

• Resolution of the romantic and main story conflict

• Reflection on the journey and growth of the characters

Character Development Sheet

Character Names: _____ / _____

• Nicknames: _____ / _____

• Ages: _____ / _____

• Occupations: _____ / _____

• Physical Descriptions: _____ / _____

• Distinguishing Features (e.g., scars, tattoos):

_____ / _____

Backstory

• Family Background: _____ / _____

• Education & Career Path: _____ / _____

• Significant Past Events: _____ / _____

• Socioeconomic Status: _____ / _____

Personality

• Dominant Traits: _____ / _____

• Fears: _____ / _____

• Desires: _____ / _____

• Hobbies/Interests: _____ / _____

• Habits (good and bad): _____ / _____

• Values & Beliefs: _____ / _____

Relationships

• Current Family Dynamics: _____ / _____

• Friendships: _____ / _____

• Past Romantic Relationships: _____

Goals

• Personal Aspirations: _____ / _____

• Professional Ambitions: _____ / _____

• Romantic Desires: _____ / _____

Conflict

• Internal Conflicts (psychological struggles, fears, uncertainties):

_____

_____

• External Conflicts (with other characters, society, environment):

_____

_____

Character Arc

• Beginning State (personality, situation at the story's start):

_____

_____

• Growth Points (key moments of change):

_____

_____

• End State (transformation or realization by the end):

_____

_____

Dialogue Style

• Speech Patterns (formal, casual, idiosyncratic phrases):

_____ / _____

• Voice (how the character's personality is reflected in dialogue):

_____ / _____

Notes

The Prompt

Two former camp best friends return as counselors years later. They find a buried time capsule full of contents. How does this rekindle a possible romance?

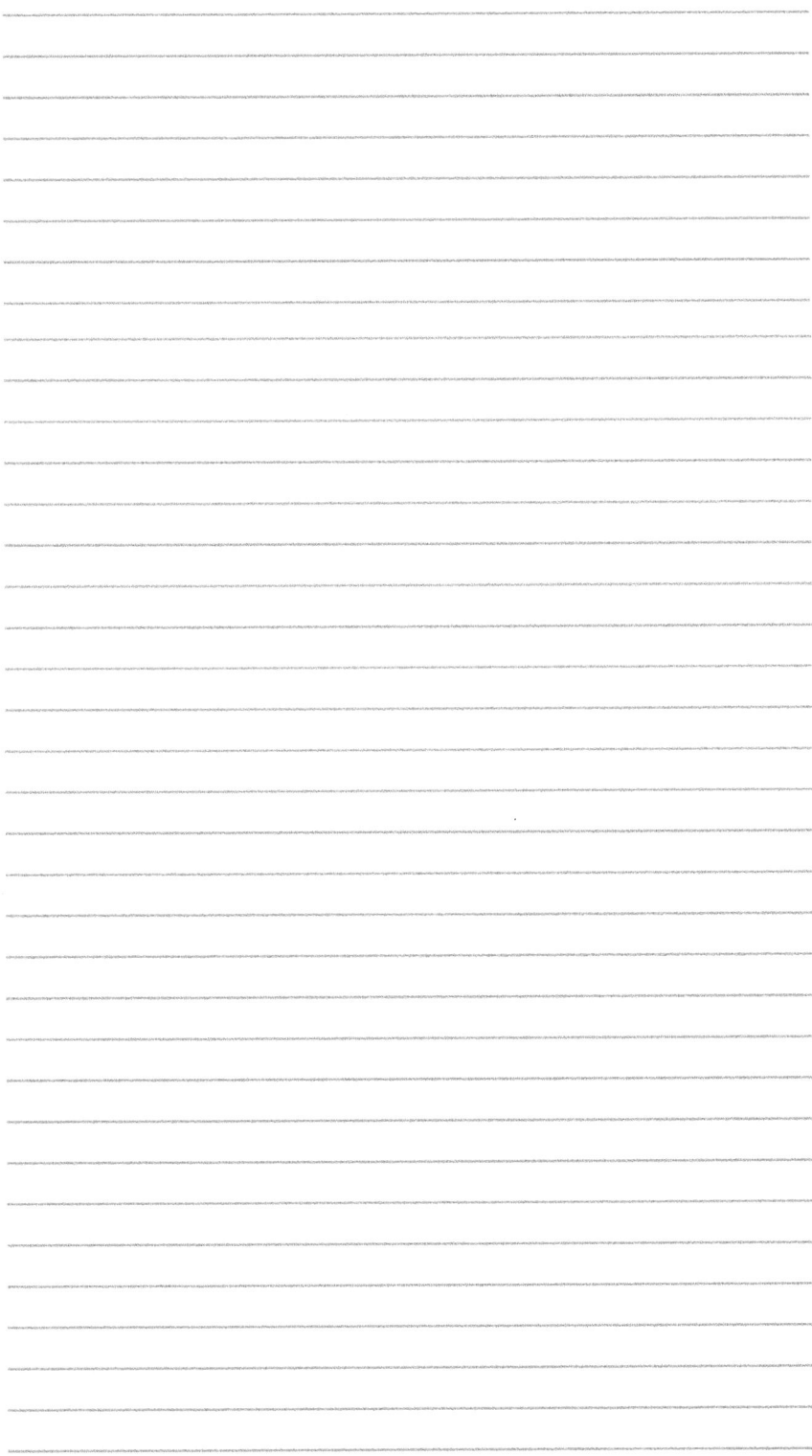

Romantic Suspense

Dive into the thrilling and heart-pounding world of Romantic Suspense, where the stakes of both love and danger are high. This subgenre combines the intrigue of a suspense or thriller novel with a central love story, creating a narrative where romance and suspense intensify each other. Characters in these stories often find themselves in perilous situations, from criminal conspiracies to mysterious circumstances, where trust, betrayal, and passion intermingle.

Key Elements:

- <u>Blend of Romance and Danger</u>: The hallmark of Romantic Suspense is the combination of an intense romantic storyline with elements of suspense or thriller.

- <u>High-Stakes Plot</u>: These stories often involve significant danger or mystery, requiring characters to navigate treacherous situations while exploring their romantic connection.

- <u>Strong, Resilient Characters</u>: The protagonists are typically strong-willed and resourceful, needing to be capable of facing physical and emotional challenges.

Notable Works and Authors:

1. *Naked in Death* by J.D. Robb: A novel that expertly combines a murder mystery with a compelling romantic plot set in a futuristic New York City.

2. *The Witness* by Nora Roberts: A gripping tale of a young woman in hiding from her past, and the man who risks everything to protect her.

3. *Mr. Perfect* by Linda Howard: A thrilling and humorous story about a group of friends who create a list of qualities that make up the perfect man, only to find themselves targeted in a deadly game.

4. *Gone Too Far* by Suzanne Brockmann: Part of the Troubleshooters series, this book blends military drama with romance, offering a high-stakes story of love amidst dangerous operations.

5. *Killing Time* by Cindy Gerard: A fast-paced romantic suspense that combines action, intrigue, and passion as part of the One-Eyed Jacks series.

Writing Tips:

- **Balancing Romance and Suspense:** Ensure that both elements – romance and suspense – are integral to the plot. Neither should overshadow the other; instead, they should complement and enhance each other.

- **Creating Tension:** Build suspense both in the romance and the overarching danger. Use tension to keep readers engaged and invested in the outcome of both the love story and the suspenseful plot.

- **Developing Strong Characters:** Characters in Romantic Suspense need to be more than just love interests. They should be complex and capable, with skills and traits that help them navigate the suspenseful elements of the story.

- **Maintaining Pace:** Keep the story moving with a good pace. Balance quieter, romantic moments with high-intensity suspense scenes to maintain reader interest and momentum.

Plot Outline Template

Title: _____

Setting: _____

Theme: _____

Act 1: Setup

• Introduction to Characters: _____

• Inciting Incident: _____

• Establishing Stakes: _____

Key Elements:

• Initial attraction or conflict

• Setting the tone and pace

Act 2: The Confrontation

• Deepening Complications: _____

• Midpoint: _____

• Build-Up to Crisis: _____

Key Elements:

• The evolution of the romantic relationship

• The introduction of secondary conflicts or subplots

Act 3: The Resolution

• Climax: _____

• Falling Action: _____

• Denouement/Conclusion: _____

Key Elements:

• Resolution of the romantic and main story conflict

• Reflection on the journey and growth of the characters

Character Development Sheet

Character Names: _____ / _____

• Nicknames: _____ / _____

• Ages: _____ / _____

• Occupations: _____ / _____

• Physical Descriptions: _____ / _____

• Distinguishing Features (e.g., scars, tattoos):

_____ / _____

Backstory

• Family Background: _____ / _____

• Education & Career Path: _____ / _____

• Significant Past Events: _____ / _____

• Socioeconomic Status: _____ / _____

Personality

• Dominant Traits: _____ / _____

• Fears: _____ / _____

• Desires: _____ / _____

• Hobbies/Interests: _____ / _____

• Habits (good and bad): _____ / _____

• Values & Beliefs: _____ / _____

Relationships

• Current Family Dynamics: _____ / _____

• Friendships: _____ / _____

• Past Romantic Relationships: _____

Goals

• Personal Aspirations: _____ / _____

• Professional Ambitions: _____ / _____

• Romantic Desires: _____ / _____

Conflict

• Internal Conflicts (psychological struggles, fears, uncertainties):

_____

_____

• External Conflicts (with other characters, society, environment):

_____

_____

Character Arc

• Beginning State (personality, situation at the story's start):

_____

_____

• Growth Points (key moments of change):

_____

_____

• End State (transformation or realization by the end):

_____

_____

Dialogue Style

• Speech Patterns (formal, casual, idiosyncratic phrases):

_____ / _____

• Voice (how the character's personality is reflected in dialogue):

_____ / _____

Notes

The Prompt

A writer looking for subjects for an upcoming story, interviews a mysterious stranger willing to expose a secret that will put the both of them in danger.

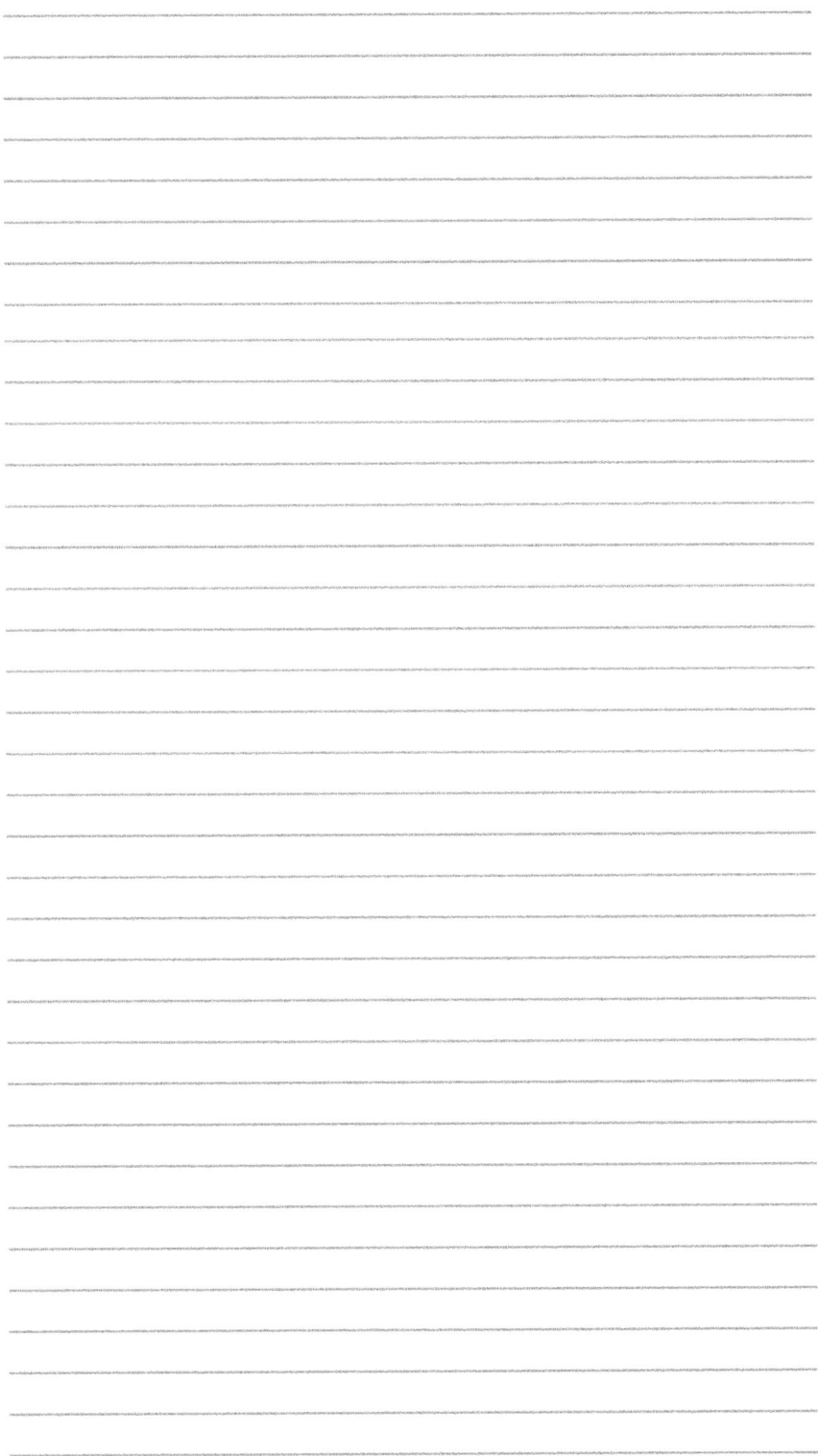

Paranormal Romance

Enter the mystical and otherworldly realm of Paranormal Romance, where the boundaries of reality blend with the supernatural. This subgenre infuses elements of fantasy, horror, and science fiction with romantic themes, creating a captivating tapestry of love stories that transcend the ordinary. From vampires and werewolves to witches and ghosts, Paranormal Romance explores romantic relationships in a world where the supernatural is a part of everyday life.

Key Elements:

- **Supernatural Beings and Worlds:** Central to this genre are characters with supernatural abilities or origins, and settings that often include elements beyond the natural world.

- **Blend of Romance and Fantasy:** While the core of these stories is the romantic relationship, the fantasy elements are integral and not just a backdrop.

- **Exploration of Forbidden or Unusual Love:** Often, these stories involve romances that defy conventional norms, such as those between humans and supernatural beings.

Notable Works and Authors:

1. *Twilight* by Stephenie Meyer: A seminal series in the genre, known for its romance between a vampire and a human.

2. *A Discovery of Witches* by Deborah Harkness: Combines history, magic, and romance in a story about a witch and a vampire uncovering secrets in an ancient manuscript.

3. *Dark Lover* by J.R. Ward: The first book in the Black Dagger Brotherhood series, featuring a band of vampire warriors and their romantic encounters.

4. *Dead Until Dark* by Charlaine Harris: The novel that introduced Sookie Stackhouse and her vampire lover, spawning the popular "True Blood" TV series.

5. *Hush, Hush* by Becca Fitzpatrick: A story about a girl who falls in love with a fallen angel, blending themes of danger and desire.

Writing Tips:

- **Create Believable Supernatural Elements:** While incorporating supernatural aspects, ground them in a reality that readers can believe and invest in.

- **Develop Multi-Dimensional Characters:** Whether your characters are vampires, werewolves, or other supernatural beings, they should have depth, desires, and conflicts like any human character.

- **Balance World-Building with Romance:** Ensure that the development of the romantic relationship and the fantasy world-building complement each other, with neither overshadowing the other.

- **Unique Take on Common Tropes:** Given the popularity of certain tropes in Paranormal Romance (e.g., vampire love stories), try to find a unique angle or fresh approach to stand out.

Plot Outline Template

Title: _____

Setting: _____

Theme: _____

Act 1: Setup

• Introduction to Characters: _____

• Inciting Incident: _____

• Establishing Stakes: _____

Key Elements:

• Initial attraction or conflict

• Setting the tone and pace

Act 2: The Confrontation

• Deepening Complications: _____

• Midpoint: _____

• Build-Up to Crisis: _____

Key Elements:

• The evolution of the romantic relationship

• The introduction of secondary conflicts or subplots

Act 3: The Resolution

• Climax: _____

• Falling Action: _____

• Denouement/Conclusion: _____

Key Elements:

• Resolution of the romantic and main story conflict

• Reflection on the journey and growth of the characters

Character Development Sheet

Character Names: _____ / _____

• Nicknames: _____ / _____

• Ages: _____ / _____

• Occupations: _____ / _____

• Physical Descriptions: _____ / _____

• Distinguishing Features (e.g., scars, tattoos):

_____ / _____

Backstory

• Family Background: _____ / _____

• Education & Career Path: _____ / _____

• Significant Past Events: _____ / _____

• Socioeconomic Status: _____ / _____

Personality

• Dominant Traits: _____ / _____

• Fears: _____ / _____

• Desires: _____ / _____

• Hobbies/Interests: _____ / _____

• Habits (good and bad): _____ / _____

• Values & Beliefs: _____ / _____

Relationships

• Current Family Dynamics: _____ / _____

• Friendships: _____ / _____

• Past Romantic Relationships: _____

Goals

• Personal Aspirations: _____ / _____

• Professional Ambitions: _____ / _____

• Romantic Desires: _____ / _____

Conflict

• Internal Conflicts (psychological struggles, fears, uncertainties):

_____

_____

• External Conflicts (with other characters, society, environment):

_____

_____

Character Arc

• Beginning State (personality, situation at the story's start):

_____

_____

• Growth Points (key moments of change):

_____

_____

• End State (transformation or realization by the end):

_____

_____

Dialogue Style

• Speech Patterns (formal, casual, idiosyncratic phrases):

_____ / _____

• Voice (how the character's personality is reflected in dialogue):

_____ / _____

Notes

The Prompt

Pair a being from the supernatural world with one from the natural world to form an unlikely alliance as they navigate their mission. Create a love that transcends the laws of their existence.

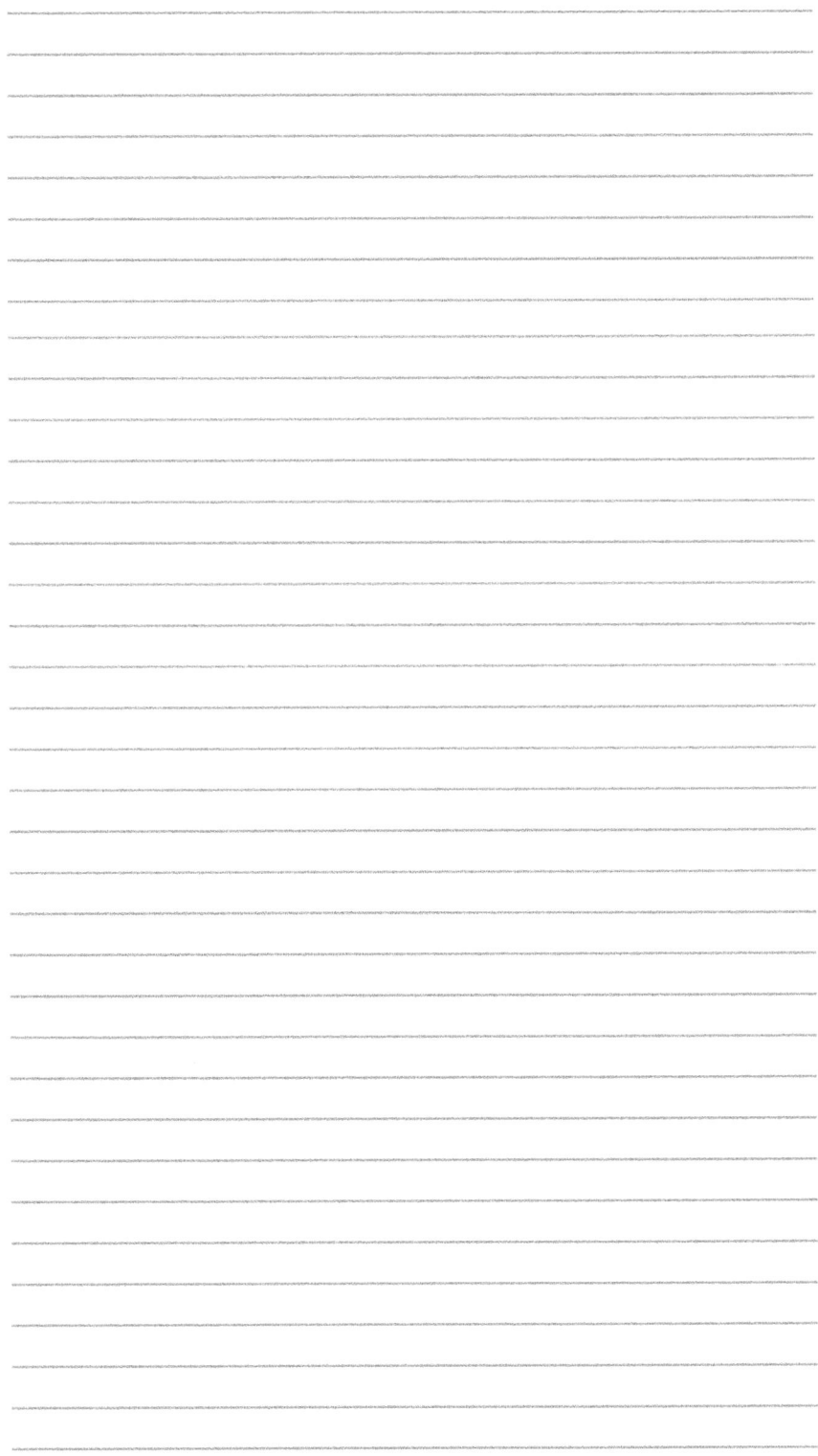

Fantasy Romance

Fantasy Romance invites readers into worlds where the enchantment of fantasy meets romantic love. This subgenre blends elements of magical and mythical settings with emotionally charged love stories, creating a space where anything is possible, and love transcends the ordinary boundaries of reality. In these tales, the fantastical elements are not just a backdrop but are integral to the plot and the development of the romantic relationship.

Key Elements:

- <u>Magical and Mythical Settings</u>: These stories often take place in richly imagined worlds filled with magic, mythical creatures, and otherworldly phenomena.

- <u>Integration of Fantasy and Romance</u>: The fantasy elements are deeply intertwined with the romance, often playing a crucial role in the development of the relationship.

- <u>Epic Narratives</u>: Many Fantasy Romance stories involve epic quests or adventures, with the romance unfolding amidst these grand narratives.

Notable Works and Authors:

1. *A Court of Thorns and Roses* by Sarah J. Maas: A series that masterfully blends romance with fantasy, set in a world of faeries and ancient curses.

2. *Stardust* by Neil Gaiman: A whimsical and enchanting tale that combines elements of adventure and romance in a magical setting.

3. *Daughter of Smoke and Bone* by Laini Taylor: A beautifully written tale of a girl caught in a war between angels and demons, entangled in a star-crossed romance.

4. *The Night Circus* by Erin Morgenstern: Set against the backdrop of a magical circus, this novel weaves a mesmerizing story of an impossible love bound by a magical competition.

5. *Kushiel's Dart* by Jacqueline Carey: An epic saga that combines intricate political intrigue with a deep and complex romantic plot in a richly detailed fantasy world.

Writing Tips:

- **Rich World-Building:** Develop a compelling fantasy world with its own rules, cultures, and history. This setting should not only enchant readers but also serve as a catalyst for the romance.

- **Complex Characters:** Create characters that are well-developed and suited to a fantasy setting. Their motivations and actions should be influenced by the magical world they inhabit.

- **Intertwine Plot and Romance:** Ensure that the fantasy plot and the romantic storyline are interwoven, each propelling the other forward. The challenges and conflicts in the fantasy world should directly impact the romantic relationship.

- **Unique Magical Elements:** Incorporate unique magical or mythical elements that enhance the romantic storyline, offering new possibilities for conflicts, connections, and character growth.

Plot Outline Template

Title: _____

Setting: _____

Theme: _____

Act 1: Setup

• Introduction to Characters: _____

• Inciting Incident: _____

• Establishing Stakes: _____

Key Elements:

• Initial attraction or conflict

• Setting the tone and pace

Act 2: The Confrontation

• Deepening Complications: _____

• Midpoint: _____

• Build-Up to Crisis: _____

Key Elements:

• The evolution of the romantic relationship

• The introduction of secondary conflicts or subplots

Act 3: The Resolution

• Climax: _____

• Falling Action: _____

• Denouement/Conclusion: _____

Key Elements:

• Resolution of the romantic and main story conflict

• Reflection on the journey and growth of the characters

Character Development Sheet

Character Names: _____ / _____

• Nicknames: _____ / _____

• Ages: _____ / _____

• Occupations: _____ / _____

• Physical Descriptions: _____ / _____

• Distinguishing Features (e.g., scars, tattoos):

_____ / _____

Backstory

• Family Background: _____ / _____

• Education & Career Path: _____ / _____

• Significant Past Events: _____ / _____

• Socioeconomic Status: _____ / _____

Personality

• Dominant Traits: _____ / _____

• Fears: _____ / _____

• Desires: _____ / _____

• Hobbies/Interests: _____ / _____

• Habits (good and bad): _____ / _____

• Values & Beliefs: _____ / _____

Relationships

• Current Family Dynamics: _____ / _____

• Friendships: _____ / _____

• Past Romantic Relationships: _____

Goals

• Personal Aspirations: _____ / _____

• Professional Ambitions: _____ / _____

• Romantic Desires: _____ / _____

Conflict

• Internal Conflicts (psychological struggles, fears, uncertainties):

_____

_____

• External Conflicts (with other characters, society, environment):

_____

_____

Character Arc

• Beginning State (personality, situation at the story's start):

_____

_____

• Growth Points (key moments of change):

_____

_____

• End State (transformation or realization by the end):

_____

_____

Dialogue Style

• Speech Patterns (formal, casual, idiosyncratic phrases):

_____ / _____

• Voice (how the character's personality is reflected in dialogue):

_____ / _____

Notes

The Prompt

When a spell mistakenly binds a wandering mage to a mystical forest guardian, their journey to unravel the magic leads to a love that blurs the boundaries between their worlds.

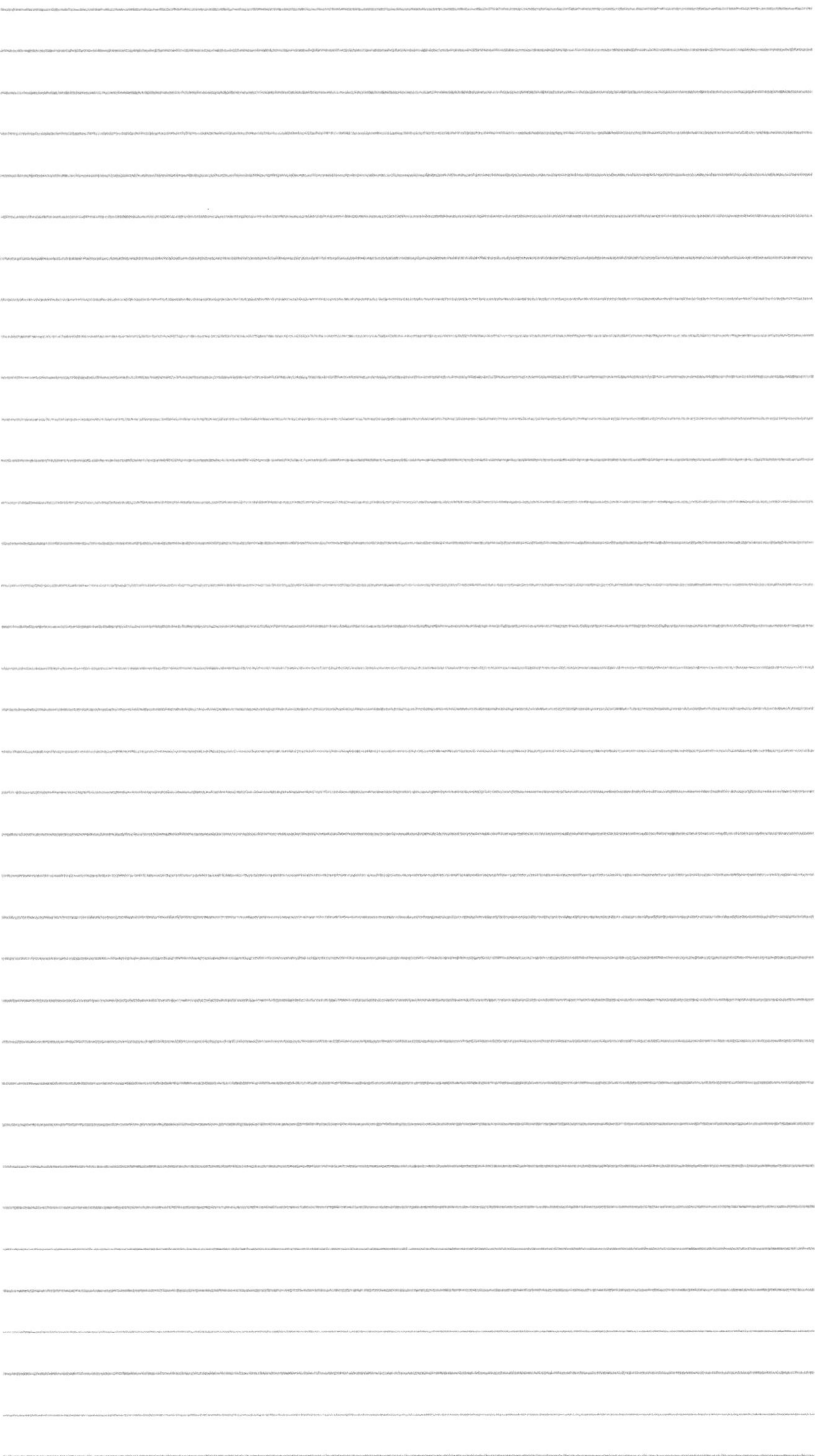

Science Fiction Romance

Take a journey through Science Fiction Romance, where the boundless possibilities of science fiction merge with the emotional depth of romantic storytelling. This subgenre explores love against a backdrop of advanced technology, space exploration, time travel, and other futuristic concepts. Sci-Fi Romance stretches the imagination, creating narratives where the relationship is as much about exploring new worlds and ideas as it is about exploring the hearts of the characters.

Key Elements:

- Futuristic or Technological Setting: Settings in Sci-Fi Romance often include advanced technologies, spacefaring civilizations, or dystopian futures.

- Integration of Sci-Fi and Romance: The science fiction elements should be integral to the plot and directly impact the romantic relationship, whether through challenges, adventures, or the nature of the world the characters inhabit.

- Themes of Exploration and Discovery: These stories often involve themes of exploration, not just of space and technology, but also of human relationships and emotions in these unique settings.

Notable Works and Authors:

1. *Shards of Honor* by Lois McMaster Bujold: Part of the Vorkosigan Saga, this novel combines space opera with a profound love story.

2. *These Broken Stars* by Amie Kaufman and Meagan Spooner: A story about survival and love on a deserted planet, blending science fiction with elements of star-crossed romance.

3. *The Time Traveler's Wife* by Audrey Niffenegger: A unique blend of time travel and deep emotional connection, exploring a complex and bittersweet love story.

4. *Cinder* by Marissa Meyer: A futuristic retelling of Cinderella, set in a world with cyborgs and lunar colonies, where a mechanic and a prince find love in unexpected circumstances.

5. *Bonds of Brass* by Emily Skrutskie: Set in a riveting space opera universe, this book features a romance that develops amidst galactic politics and rebellion.

Writing Tips:

- **Balanced Storytelling:** Ensure that both the science fiction and romance elements are given equal weight. The technological or futuristic aspects should complement and enhance the romantic plot, not overshadow it.

- **Creating Believable Futures:** Develop a well-thought-out futuristic world with plausible advancements in technology and society. This setting should serve as a compelling backdrop for the romance.

- **Character Depth and Development:** In a world of advanced technology and new frontiers, focus on humanizing your characters. Their emotions, relationships, and growth should remain relatable and authentic.

- **Incorporate Sci-Fi Themes into the Romance:** Use classic sci-fi themes like time travel, artificial intelligence, or space exploration as integral parts of the relationship development and conflict.

Plot Outline Template

Title: _____

Setting: _____

Theme: _____

Act 1: Setup

• Introduction to Characters: _____

• Inciting Incident: _____

• Establishing Stakes: _____

Key Elements:

• Initial attraction or conflict

• Setting the tone and pace

Act 2: The Confrontation

• Deepening Complications: _____

• Midpoint: _____

• Build-Up to Crisis: _____

Key Elements:

• The evolution of the romantic relationship

• The introduction of secondary conflicts or subplots

Act 3: The Resolution

• Climax: _____

• Falling Action: _____

• Denouement/Conclusion: _____

Key Elements:

• Resolution of the romantic and main story conflict

• Reflection on the journey and growth of the characters

Character Development Sheet

Character Names: _____ / _____

• Nicknames: _____ / _____

• Ages: _____ / _____

• Occupations: _____ / _____

• Physical Descriptions: _____ / _____

• Distinguishing Features (e.g., scars, tattoos):

_____ / _____

Backstory

• Family Background: _____ / _____

• Education & Career Path: _____ / _____

• Significant Past Events: _____ / _____

• Socioeconomic Status: _____ / _____

Personality

• Dominant Traits: _____ / _____

• Fears: _____ / _____

• Desires: _____ / _____

• Hobbies/Interests: _____ / _____

• Habits (good and bad): _____ / _____

• Values & Beliefs: _____ / _____

Relationships

• Current Family Dynamics: _____ / _____

• Friendships: _____ / _____

• Past Romantic Relationships: _____

Goals

• Personal Aspirations: _____ / _____

• Professional Ambitions: _____ / _____

• Romantic Desires: _____ / _____

Conflict

• Internal Conflicts (psychological struggles, fears, uncertainties):

_____

_____

• External Conflicts (with other characters, society, environment):

_____

_____

Character Arc

• Beginning State (personality, situation at the story's start):

_____

_____

• Growth Points (key moments of change):

_____

_____

• End State (transformation or realization by the end):

_____

_____

Dialogue Style

• Speech Patterns (formal, casual, idiosyncratic phrases):

_____ / _____

• Voice (how the character's personality is reflected in dialogue):

_____ / _____

Notes

The Prompt

A quantum pilot navigating parallel universes rescues a dimensional wanderer from a collapsing world. How does this pair form a bond that leads to romance?

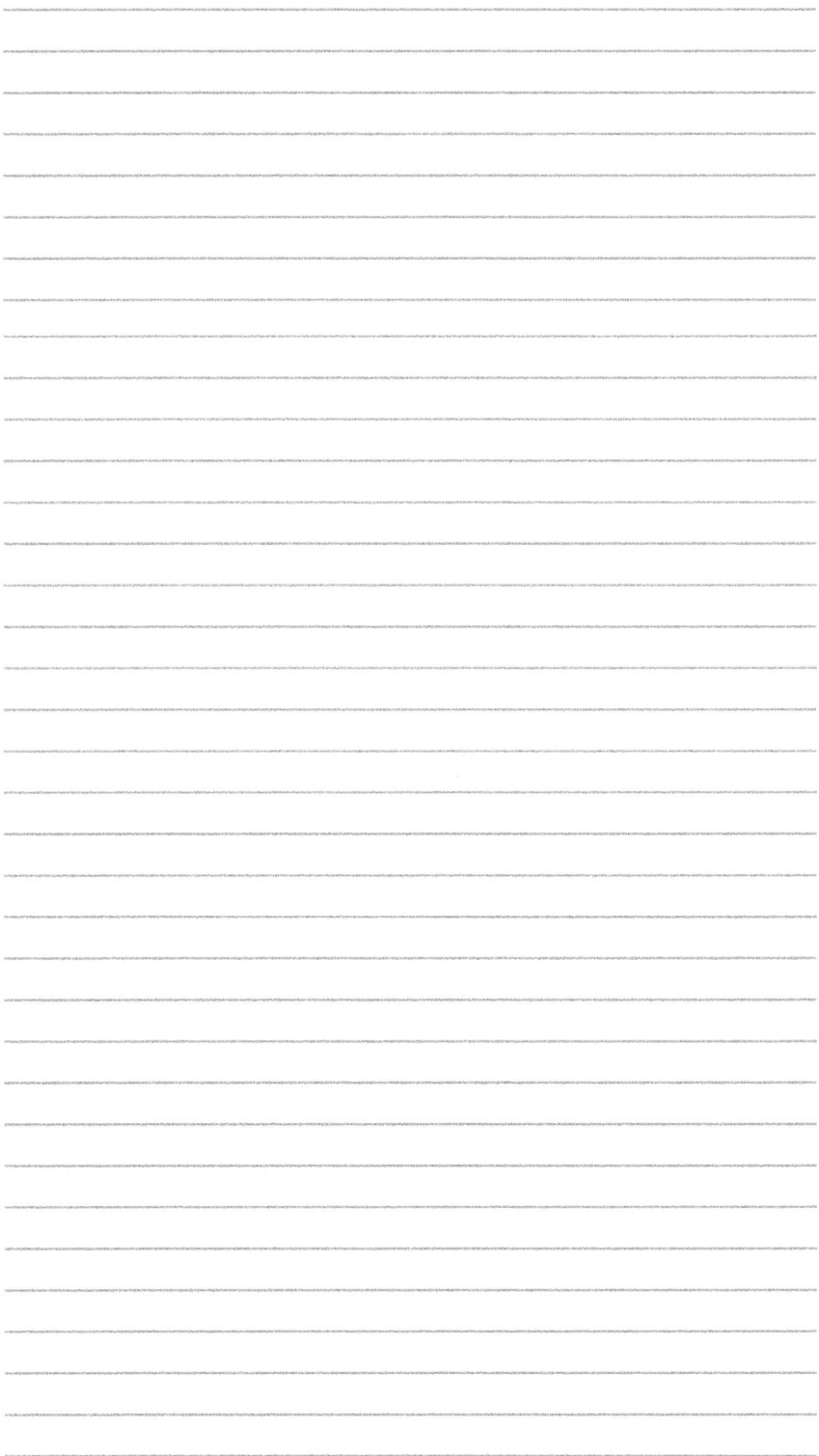

Doomed Romance

Immerse yourself in the poignant and often bittersweet world of Doomed Romance, where love stories are marked by a sense of inevitable tragedy or insurmountable obstacles. This subgenre captures the intensity of passionate love affairs destined for a heartbreaking conclusion. Often exploring themes of star-crossed lovers, forbidden relationships, or unrequited love, Doomed Romance delves into the depths of human emotion, illuminating the more melancholic aspects of love.

Key Elements:

- <u>Tragic or Forbidden Love</u>: Central to Doomed Romance is the concept of love that is hindered by external circumstances, societal norms, or personal tragedies.

- <u>Emotional Depth</u>: These stories often explore the depths of love and loss, delving into the complexities and nuances of intense emotional experiences.

- <u>Atmosphere of Melancholy</u>: A prevailing sense of melancholy or fatalism permeates these narratives, often underscored by beautiful, poignant writing.

Notable Works and Authors:

1. *Wuthering Heights* by Emily Brontë: A classic novel that epitomizes doomed love with its tumultuous and tragic story of Cathy and Heathcliff.

2. *Romeo and Juliet* by William Shakespeare: Perhaps the most famous example of star-crossed lovers, this play explores the ultimate tragedy of forbidden love.

3. *The Great Gatsby* by F. Scott Fitzgerald: A story of unrequited love and longing set against the backdrop of the Roaring Twenties.

4. *Me Before You* by Jojo Moyes: A contemporary novel that explores a deep and unlikely love, shadowed by the specter of an impossible future.

5. *Atonement* by Ian McEwan: A novel where a single act of youthful naivety drastically changes the course of several lives, leading to a love thwarted by circumstance and misunderstanding.

Writing Tips:

- **Crafting Tragic Arcs:** Develop story arcs that naturally lead to a tragic or bittersweet conclusion. The impending sense of doom should be woven seamlessly into the narrative.

- **Building Intense Relationships:** Focus on creating a deep, intense connection between the characters. Their love should be profound and compelling, making the eventual outcome all the more impactful.

- **Balancing Poignancy and Despair:** While the tone of Doomed Romance is often melancholic, balance the sorrow with moments of beauty, love, and hope.

- **Exploring Themes of Fate and Choice:** Delve into themes of destiny, choice, and the forces that pull the lovers apart. This adds depth and philosophical layers to the narrative.

Plot Outline Template

Title: _____

Setting: _____

Theme: _____

Act 1: Setup

• Introduction to Characters: _____

• Inciting Incident: _____

• Establishing Stakes: _____

Key Elements:

• Initial attraction or conflict

• Setting the tone and pace

Act 2: The Confrontation

• Deepening Complications: _____

• Midpoint: _____

• Build-Up to Crisis: _____

Key Elements:

• The evolution of the romantic relationship

• The introduction of secondary conflicts or subplots

Act 3: The Resolution

• Climax: _____

• Falling Action: _____

• Denouement/Conclusion: _____

Key Elements:

• Resolution of the romantic and main story conflict

• Reflection on the journey and growth of the characters

Character Development Sheet

Character Names: _____ / _____

• Nicknames: _____ / _____

• Ages: _____ / _____

• Occupations: _____ / _____

• Physical Descriptions: _____ / _____

• Distinguishing Features (e.g., scars, tattoos):

_____ / _____

Backstory

• Family Background: _____ / _____

• Education & Career Path: _____ / _____

• Significant Past Events: _____ / _____

• Socioeconomic Status: _____ / _____

Personality

• Dominant Traits: _____ / _____

• Fears: _____ / _____

• Desires: _____ / _____

• Hobbies/Interests: _____ / _____

• Habits (good and bad): _____ / _____

• Values & Beliefs: _____ / _____

Relationships

• Current Family Dynamics: _____ / _____

• Friendships: _____ / _____

• Past Romantic Relationships: _____

Goals

• Personal Aspirations: _____ / _____

• Professional Ambitions: _____ / _____

• Romantic Desires: _____ / _____

Conflict

• Internal Conflicts (psychological struggles, fears, uncertainties):

_____

_____

• External Conflicts (with other characters, society, environment):

_____

_____

Character Arc

• Beginning State (personality, situation at the story's start):

_____

_____

• Growth Points (key moments of change):

_____

_____

• End State (transformation or realization by the end):

_____

_____

Dialogue Style

• Speech Patterns (formal, casual, idiosyncratic phrases):

_____ / _____

• Voice (how the character's personality is reflected in dialogue):

_____ / _____

Notes

The Prompt

Two former lovers spend a day together, catching up on the lives they've led since their passionate but chaotic relationship that ended years ago. How do they realize that not all love last forever?

Erotica

Step into the bold and sensual world of Erotica, a genre that unabashedly explores the sexual aspects of relationships. This subgenre is characterized by explicit sexual scenes and themes, focusing on the physical and emotional aspects of sexual relationships. Erotica often goes beyond mere titillation, offering deeper insights into human sexuality, desires, and the complex interplay of physical and emotional intimacy.

Key Elements:

- Explicit Sexual Content: The hallmark of Erotica is its explicit depiction of sexual activities, described in a way that is integral to the characters' development and the story's progression.

- Emotional and Physical Connection: While the focus is on sexuality, the emotional and physical connections between characters are crucial, providing depth and context to the sexual encounters.

- Exploration of Desires and Fantasies: Erotica often delves into a variety of desires and fantasies, offering a space for characters (and readers) to explore different aspects of sexuality.

Notable Works and Authors:

1. *Fifty Shades of Grey* by E.L. James: Known for popularizing the genre in mainstream media, this series explores themes of desire and power dynamics within a sexual relationship.

2. *Delta of Venus* by Anaïs Nin: A classic collection of erotic short stories that delve into various aspects of human sexuality with literary flair.

3. *Bared to You* by Sylvia Day: Part of the Crossfire series, this novel delves into a passionate and obsessive relationship, marked by deep emotional connections and intense sexual experiences.

4. *Story of O* by Pauline Réage: A controversial and iconic work in the genre, known for its exploration of submission and desire.

5. *The Sleeping Beauty Quartet* by Anne Rice (writing as A.N. Roquelaure): A series of erotic novels set in a fantasy world, combining elements of retold fairy tales with explicit sexual adventures.

Writing Tips:

- **Developing Compelling Characters:** Characters in Erotica should be well-developed, with their own desires, fears, and motivations. The sexual experiences should serve to reveal different facets of their personalities.

- **Balancing Explicit Content with Storytelling:** While the sexual content is explicit, it should be balanced with strong storytelling, character development, and emotional depth.

- **Exploring Themes and Dynamics:** Use Erotica to explore various themes and dynamics, such as power play, vulnerability, and consent, adding layers to the sexual encounters.

- **Respect and Authenticity:** Approach the genre with respect and authenticity. Be mindful of how sexual encounters are depicted, ensuring they are consensual and empowering for the characters involved.

Plot Outline Template

Title: _____

Setting: _____

Theme: _____

Act 1: Setup

• Introduction to Characters: _____

• Inciting Incident: _____

• Establishing Stakes: _____

Key Elements:

• Initial attraction or conflict

• Setting the tone and pace

Act 2: The Confrontation

• Deepening Complications: _____

• Midpoint: _____

• Build-Up to Crisis: _____

Key Elements:

• The evolution of the romantic relationship

• The introduction of secondary conflicts or subplots

Act 3: The Resolution

• Climax: _____

• Falling Action: _____

• Denouement/Conclusion: _____

Key Elements:

• Resolution of the romantic and main story conflict

• Reflection on the journey and growth of the characters

Character Development Sheet

Character Names: _____ / _____

- Nicknames: _____ / _____

- Ages: _____ / _____

- Occupations: _____ / _____

- Physical Descriptions: _____ / _____

- Distinguishing Features (e.g., scars, tattoos):

  _____ / _____

Backstory

- Family Background: _____ / _____

- Education & Career Path: _____ / _____

- Significant Past Events: _____ / _____

- Socioeconomic Status: _____ / _____

Personality

- Dominant Traits: _____ / _____

- Fears: _____ / _____

- Desires: _____ / _____

- Hobbies/Interests: _____ / _____

- Habits (good and bad): _____ / _____

- Values & Beliefs: _____ / _____

Relationships

- Current Family Dynamics: _____ / _____

- Friendships: _____ / _____

- Past Romantic Relationships: _____

Goals

• Personal Aspirations: _____ / _____

• Professional Ambitions: _____ / _____

• Romantic Desires: _____ / _____

Conflict

• Internal Conflicts (psychological struggles, fears, uncertainties):

_____

_____

• External Conflicts (with other characters, society, environment):

_____

_____

Character Arc

• Beginning State (personality, situation at the story's start):

_____

_____

• Growth Points (key moments of change):

_____

_____

• End State (transformation or realization by the end):

_____

_____

Dialogue Style

• Speech Patterns (formal, casual, idiosyncratic phrases):

_____ / _____

• Voice (how the character's personality is reflected in dialogue):

_____ / _____

Notes

The Prompt

A shy individual receives an invitation to an exclusive masked erotic ball. There is anonymity, freedom, and uninhibited passion. How does the night progress and how does the night end?

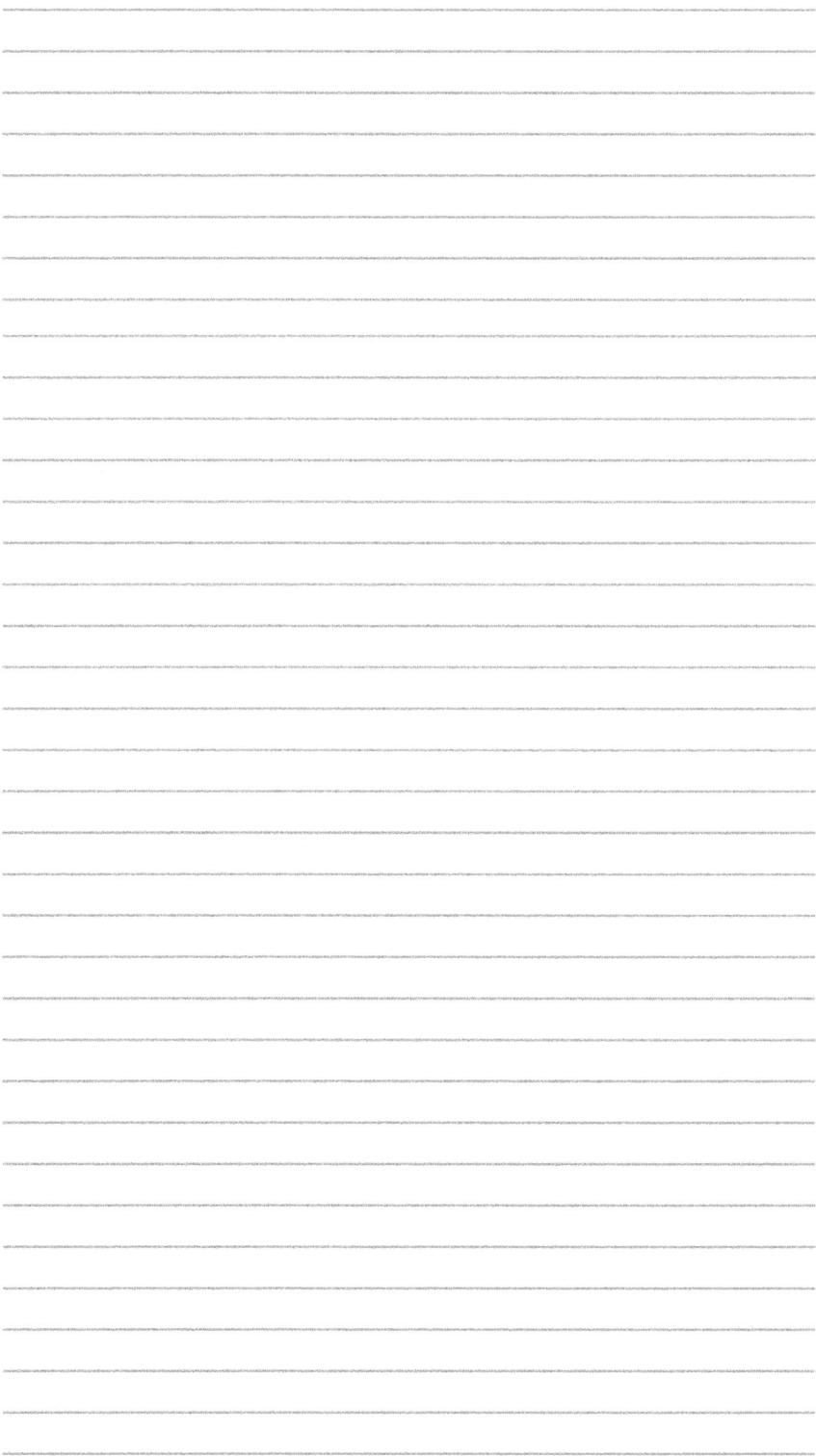

Thank You!

As we reach the end of our journey together through these prompts, I hope you've found sparks of inspiration, moments of challenge, and above all, a deeper love for the art of storytelling. If this book has played a part in your writing journey, I invite you to share your experience by leaving a review.

Your insights not only celebrate our shared passion for storytelling but also guide fellow writers to resources that could enlighten their own creative paths. Whether it's a brief note or an in-depth reflection, your feedback is a beacon for the community and a treasure for me.

Thank you for embracing the adventure of writing with me. Your engagement and support illuminate the way forward.

With warmest regards,

Mark El-Ayat

STORY PROMPTS

This book is one in a series that features various genres of story prompts. Take your creative journey to the next level with our Story Prompts books. They're designed to inspire and guide your storytelling across various genres.

Find new worlds, interesting characters, and exciting plots that are waiting for your unique voice.

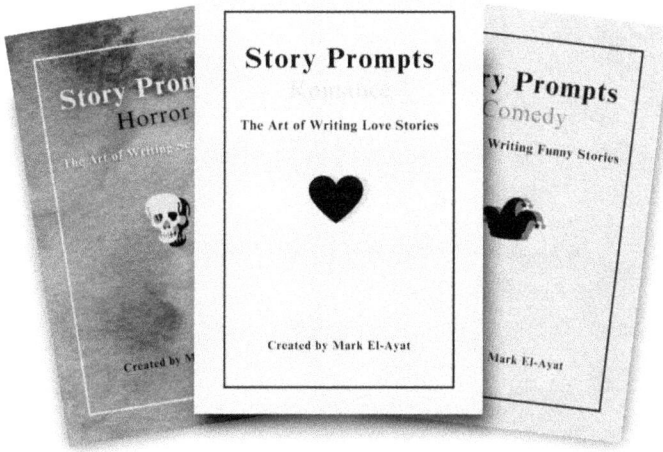

Our Story Prompts series is here to help writers at any stage, with a wide range of prompts to dive into different themes, characters, and plots. Don't stop writing! Your next amazing story starts right here!

For more information and to discover other books in the series, visit my website www.markelayat.com

www.ingramcontent.com/pod-product-compliance
Lightning Source LLC
Chambersburg PA
CBHW052116030426
42335CB00025B/3013